Planet Mandala Coloring Book

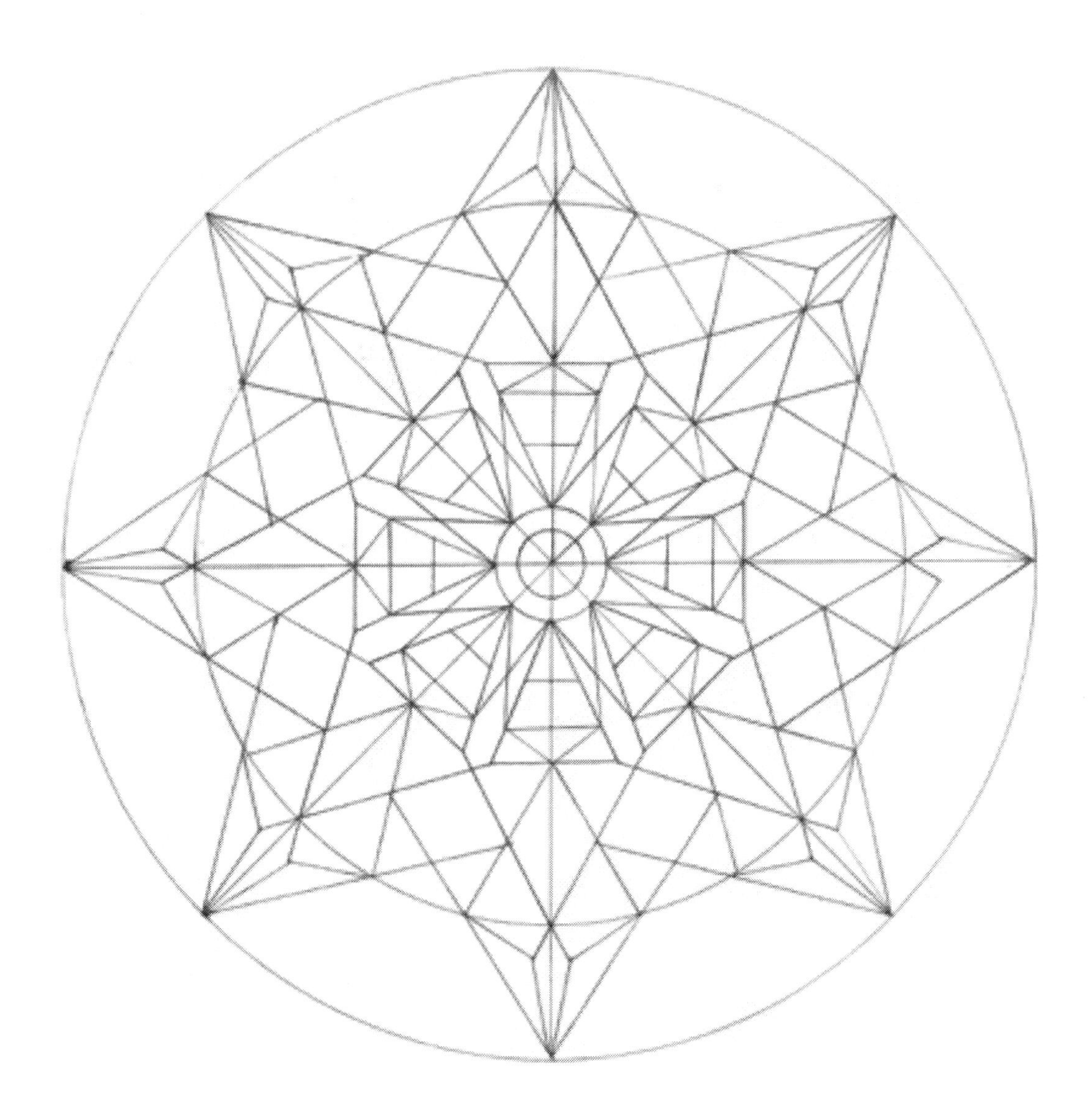

Mavis Gewant

Sacred Mother Arts

Planets, Numbers, and Colors:

For thousands of years, tantric seers have observed the powerful influence of the planets on the human spirit. Indian astrologers believe that energy is released by orbiting planets in our solar system. This energy, when directed and harnessed, can affect our lives and improve our spiritual, mental, and physical wellbeing.

Mandalas are sacred circular energy patterns that reflect our inner nature. According to the Vedic Astrology system of India, numbers and planets are connected and are associated with specific colors. An ancient number grid, called the Vedic Square, is used to create infinite shapes and patterns to form a unique mandala based on corresponding planets. By working with specific colors, this meditative painting practice will connect us to the deeper energies of the planets; creating more harmony, peace, and energy.

Number	Planet	Sign	Colors
1	Sun	Leo	Orange, Red, Yellow, Gold
2	Moon	Cancer	Light Blue, Silver, White
3	Jupiter	Pisces, Sagittarius	Yellow
4	Rahu	North Node	Earth Tones, Brown, Smokey and Muted Colors
5	Mercury	Gemini, Virgo	Green, Blue-Green
6	Venus	Taurus, Libra	White, Pastel Shades of Blue, Pink and Purple
7	Ketu	South Node	Olive Green, Grey, Smokey Colors
8	Saturn	Capricorn, Aquarius	Black, Dark Blue, Violet
9	Mars	Aries, Scorpio	Red, Coral, Red-Orange, Pink

How to use this book:
Color each mandala with the suggested colors to feel the effects of the planet's energy. Included in this book are duplicates so you can achieve a variety of color combinations.

Suggested Materials:
Colored pencils, gouache, markers. Place a heavy piece of paper behind the mandala to prevent color bleeding.

For more information and workshops on creating your own Planet Mandala:
www.sacredmotherarts.com

For more information on Numerology:
Johari, Harish. *Numerology: With Tantra, Ayurveda, and Astrology.* Destiny Books, 1990.

#1, Sun

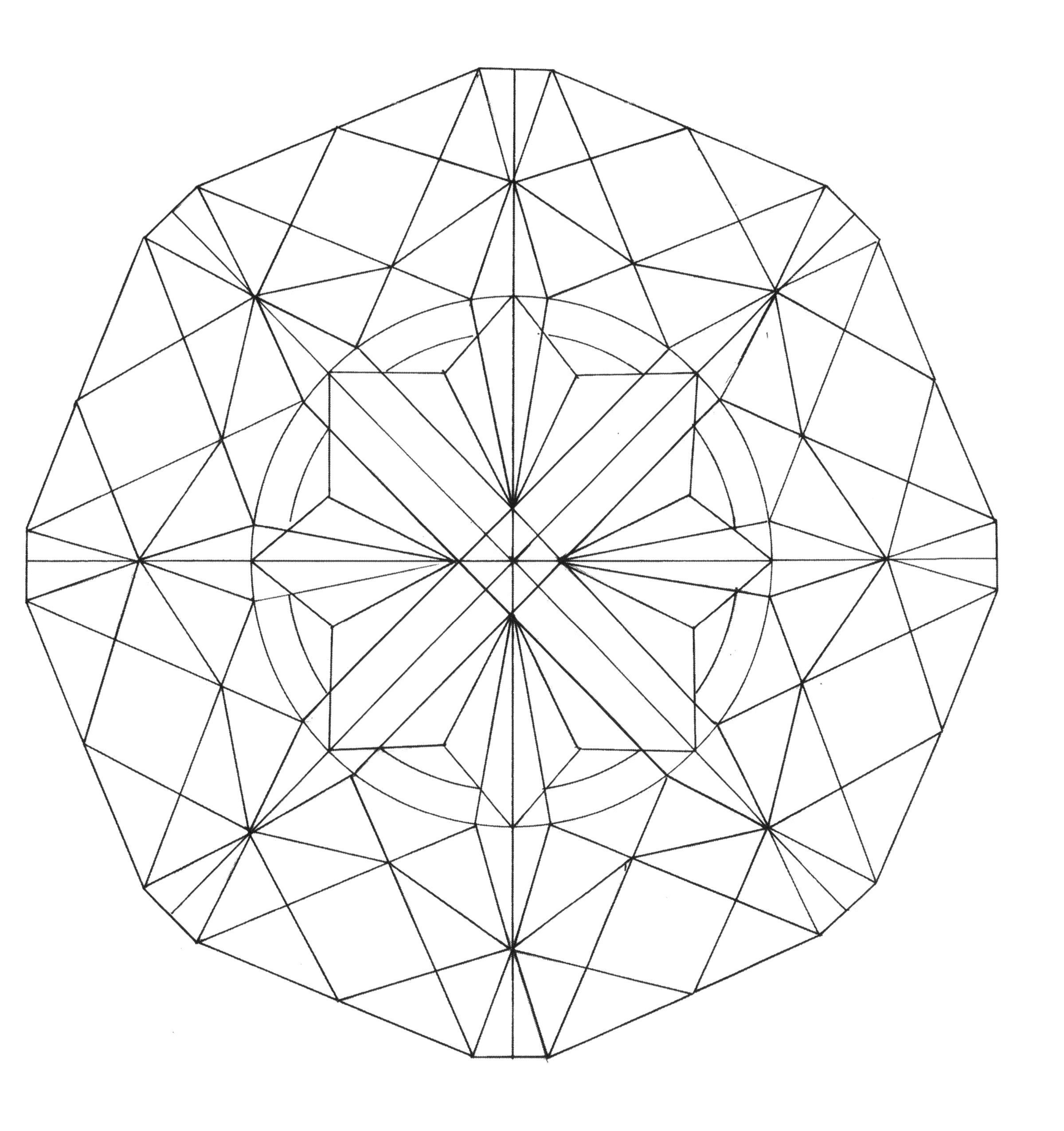

#2, Moon

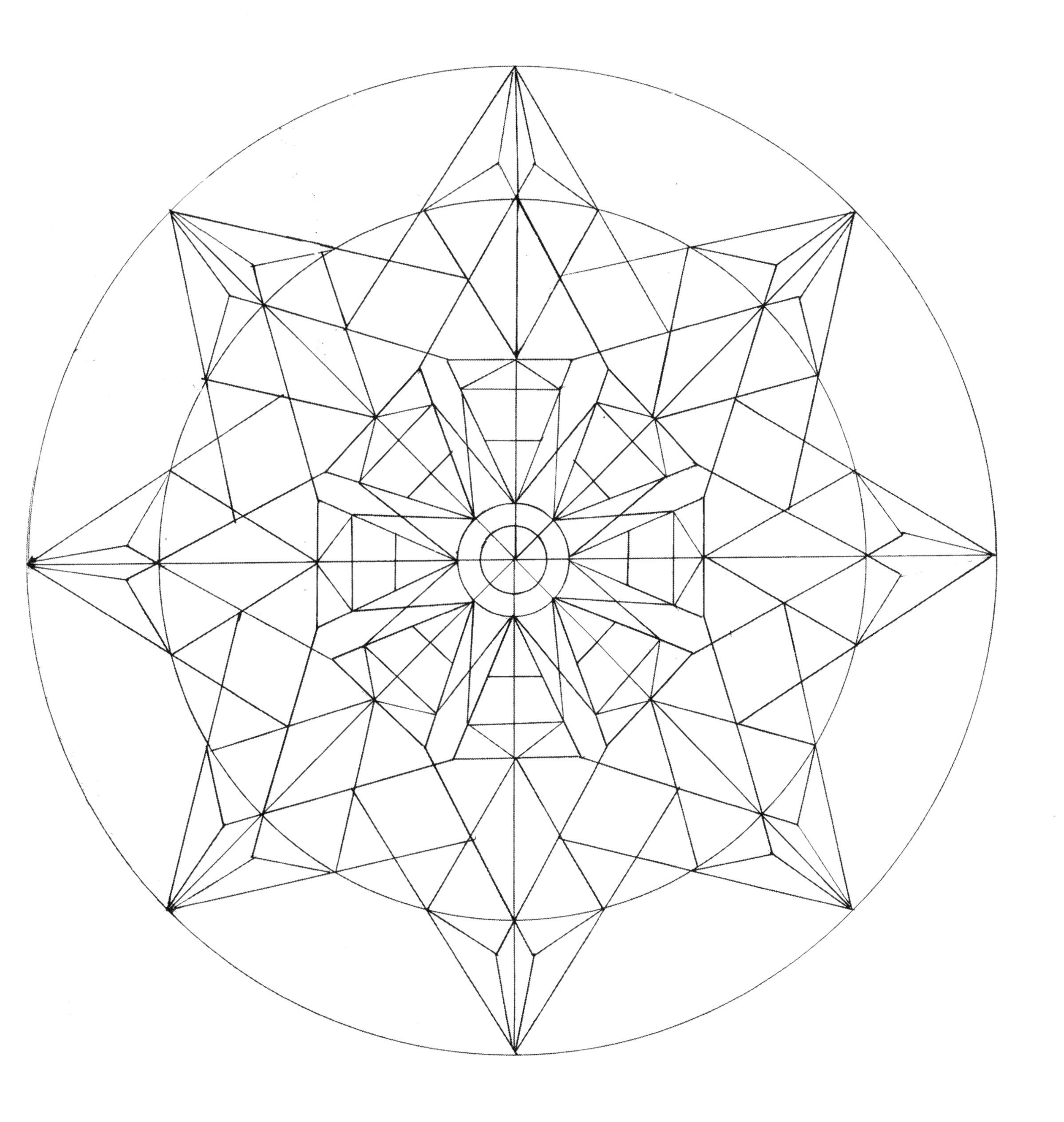

#3, Jupiter

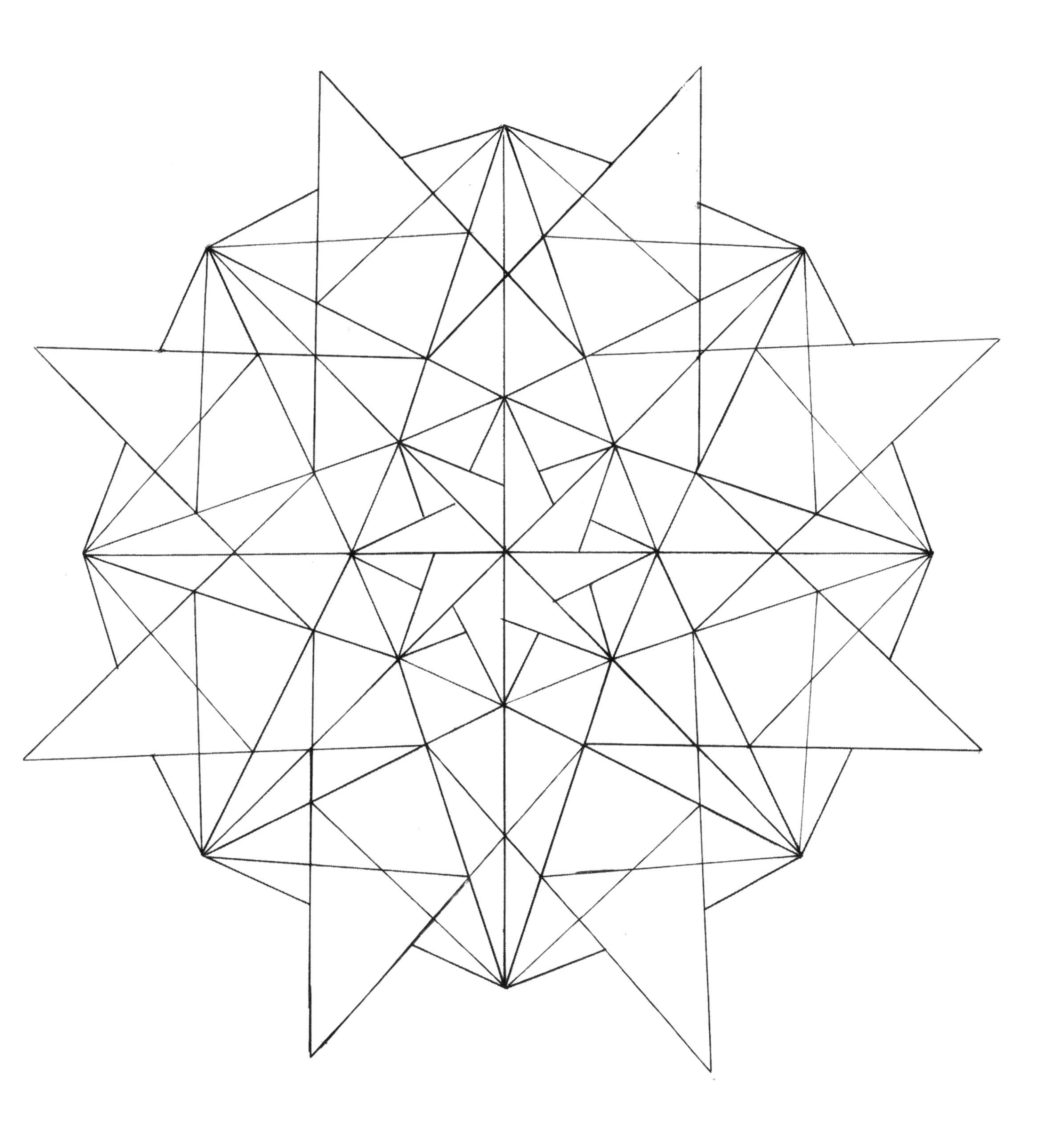

#4, Rahu

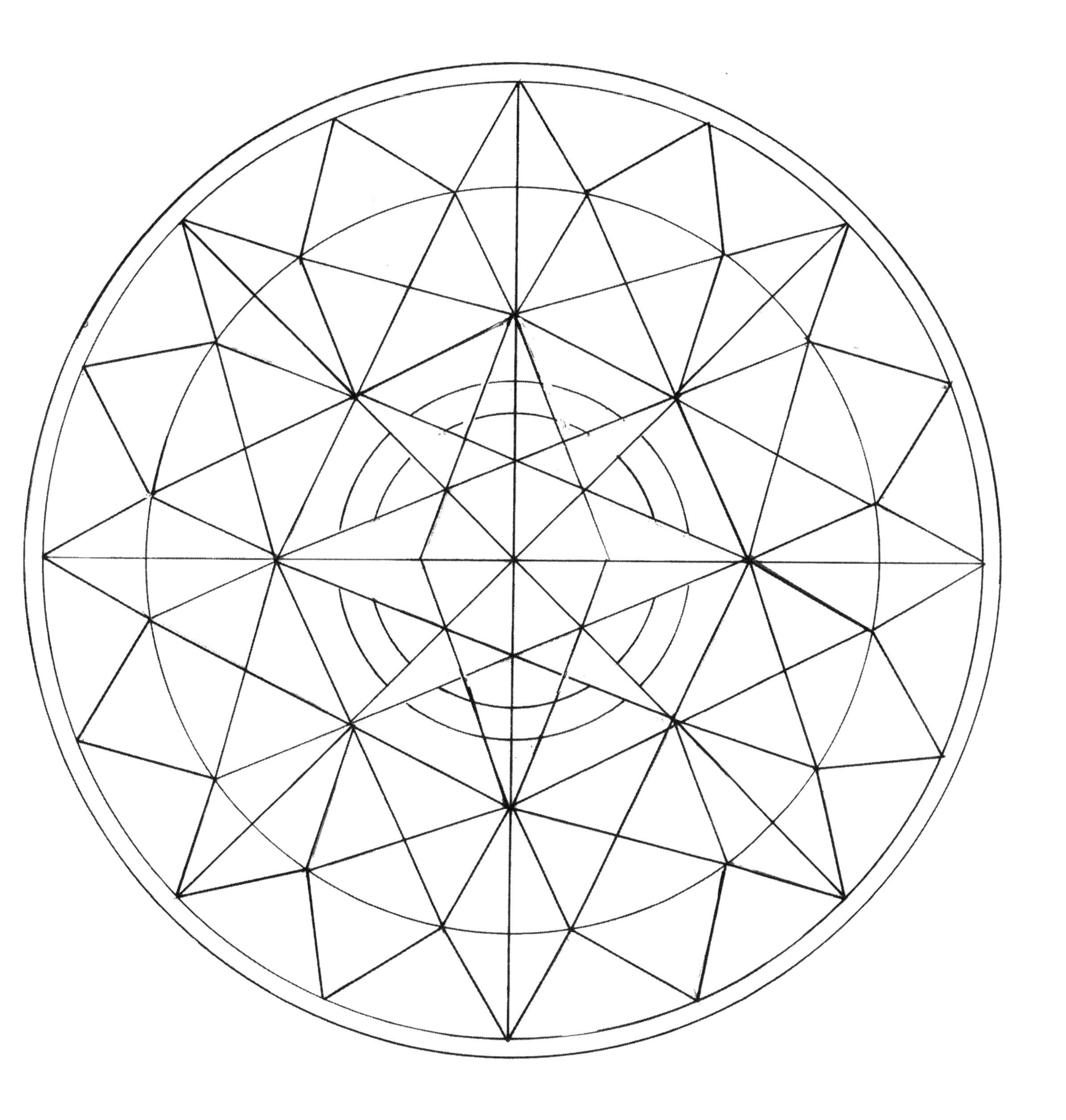

#5, Mercury

#6, Venus

#7, Ketu

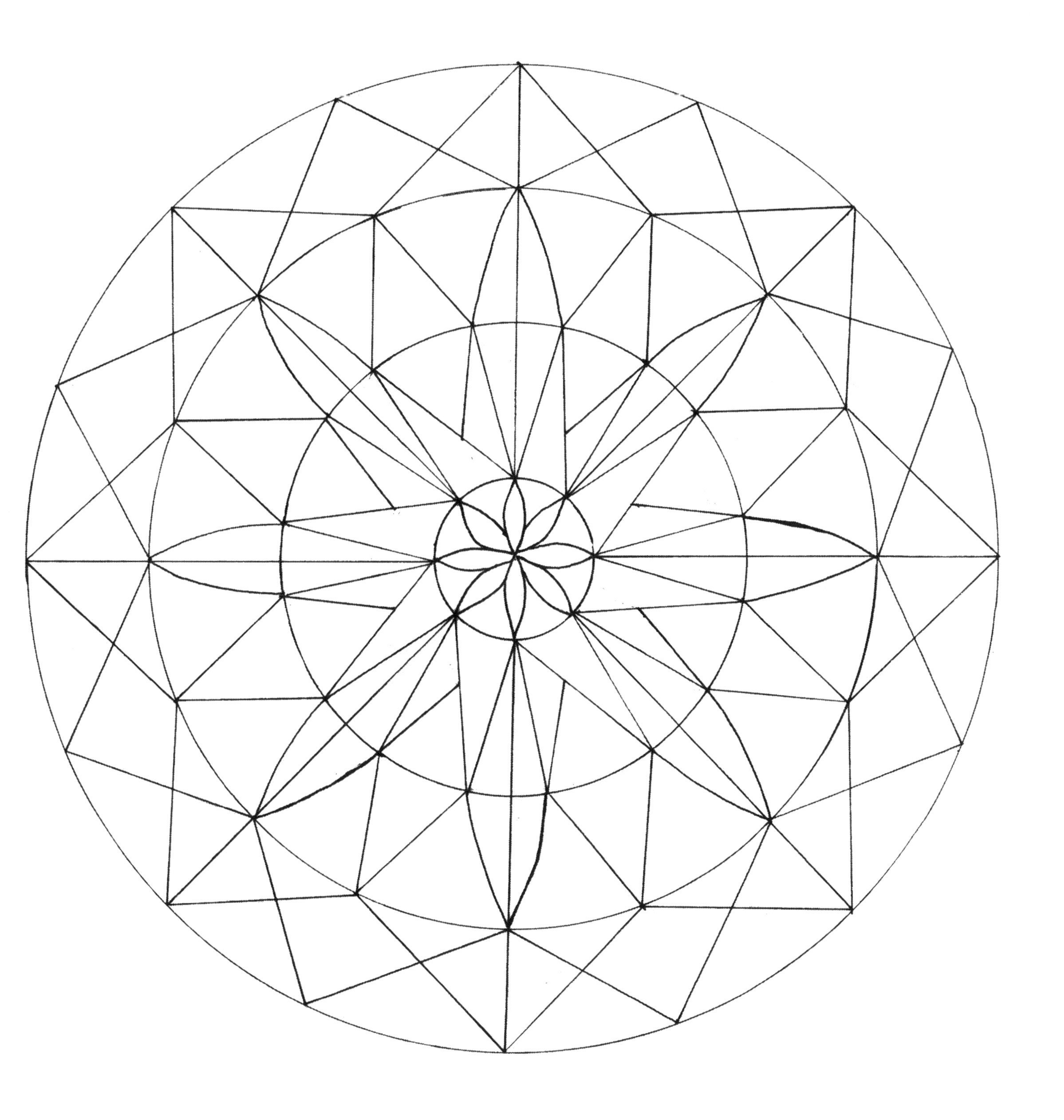

#8, Saturn

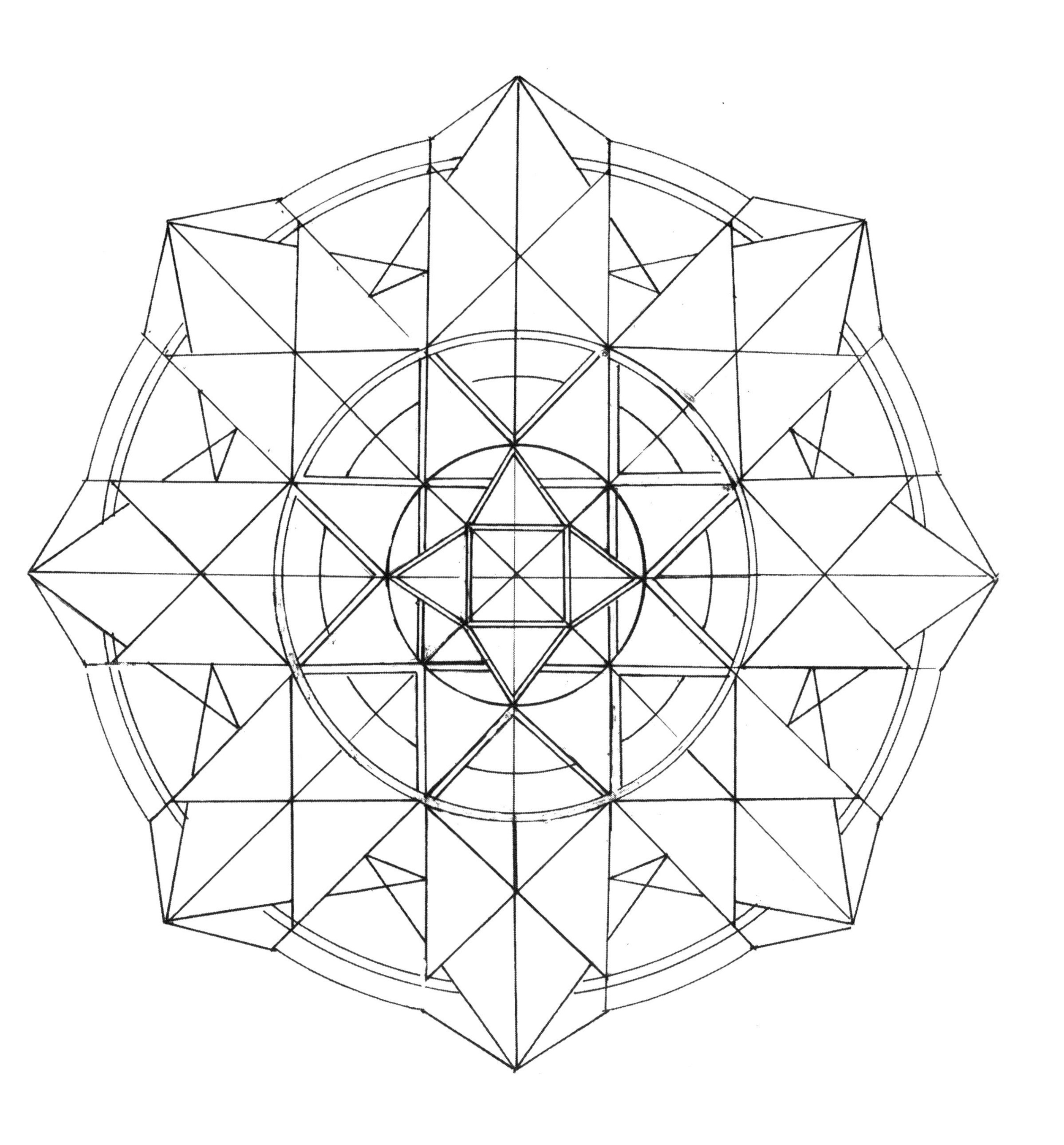

#9, Mars

#1, Sun

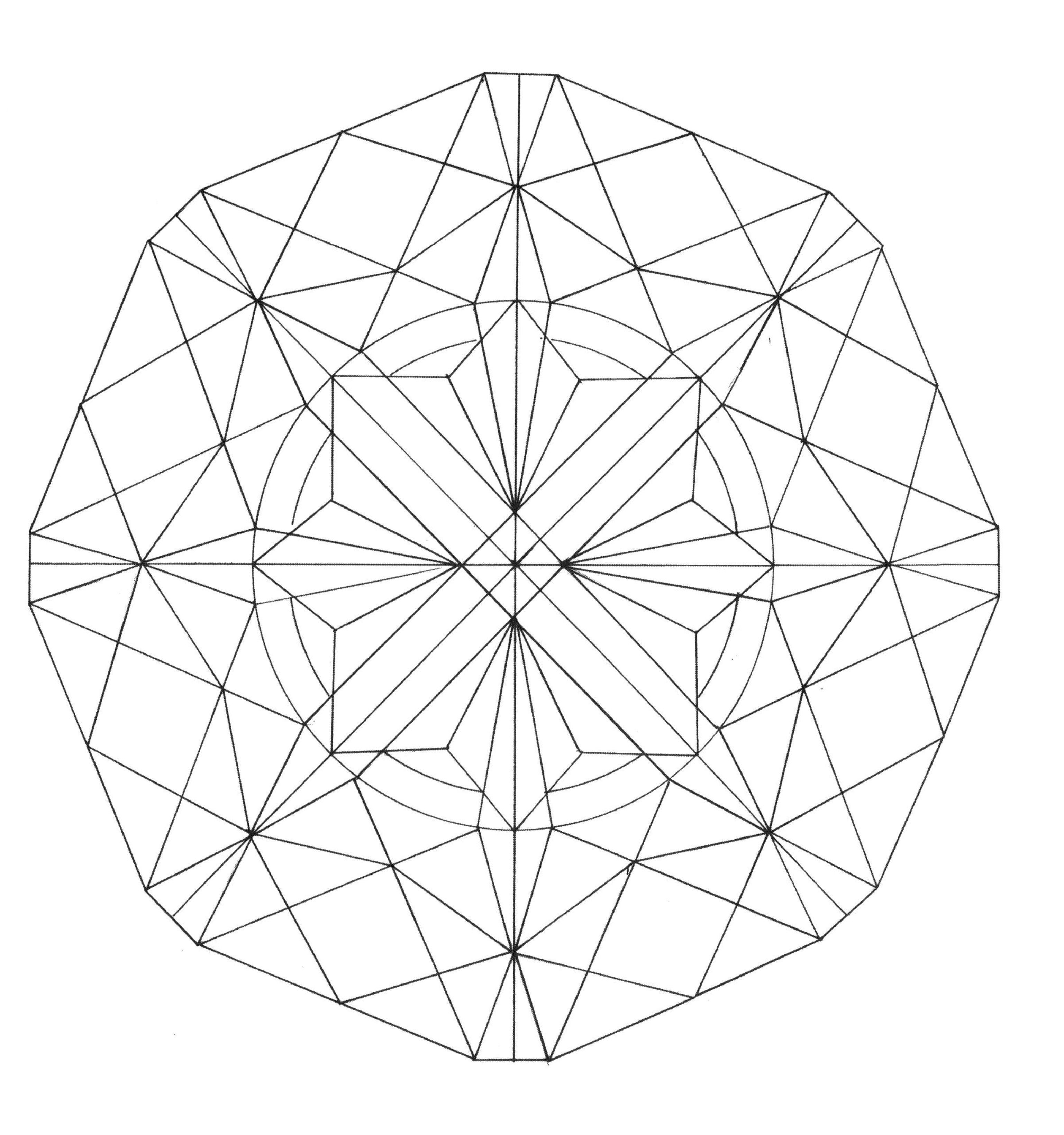

#2, Moon

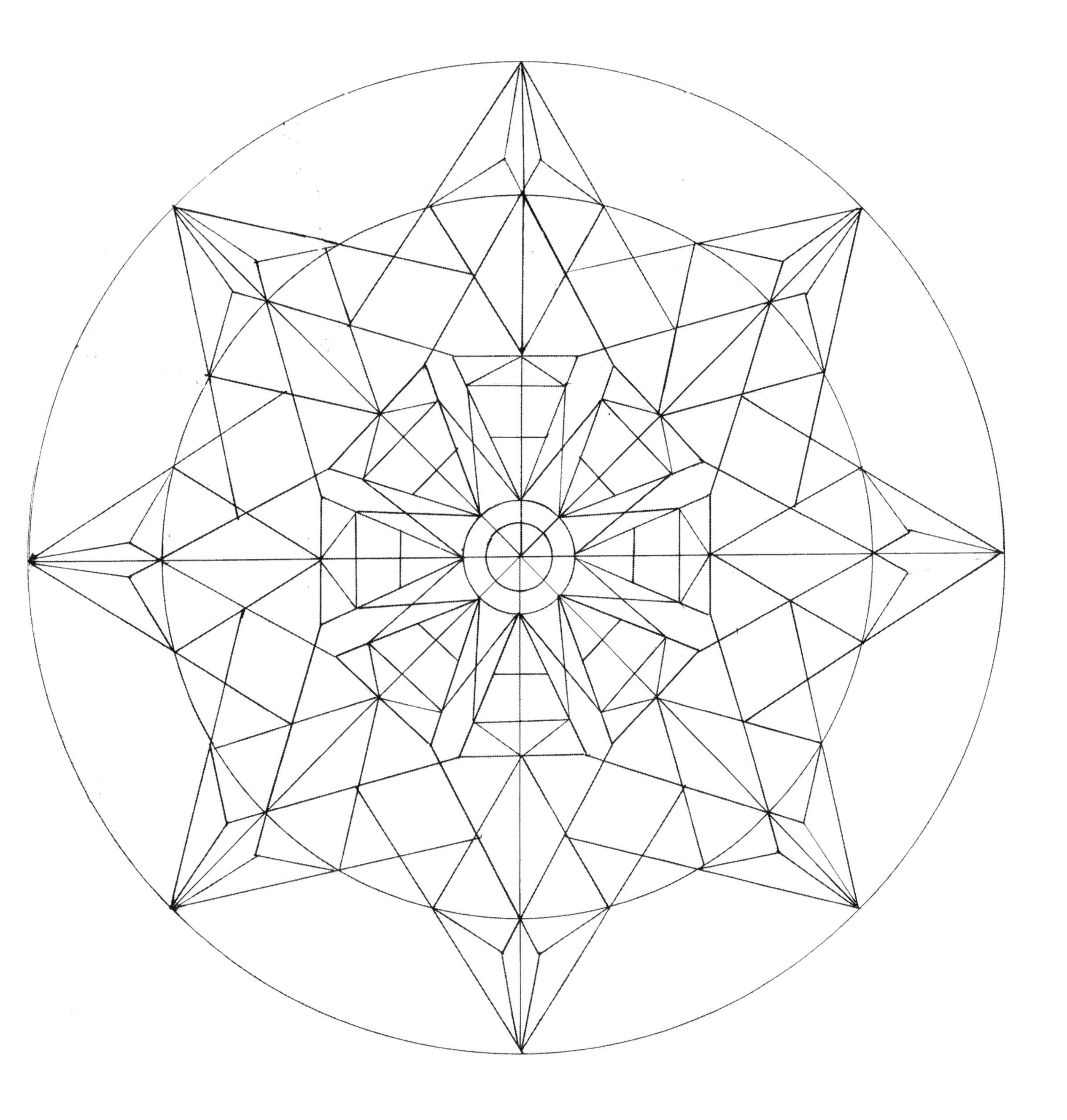

#3, Jupiter

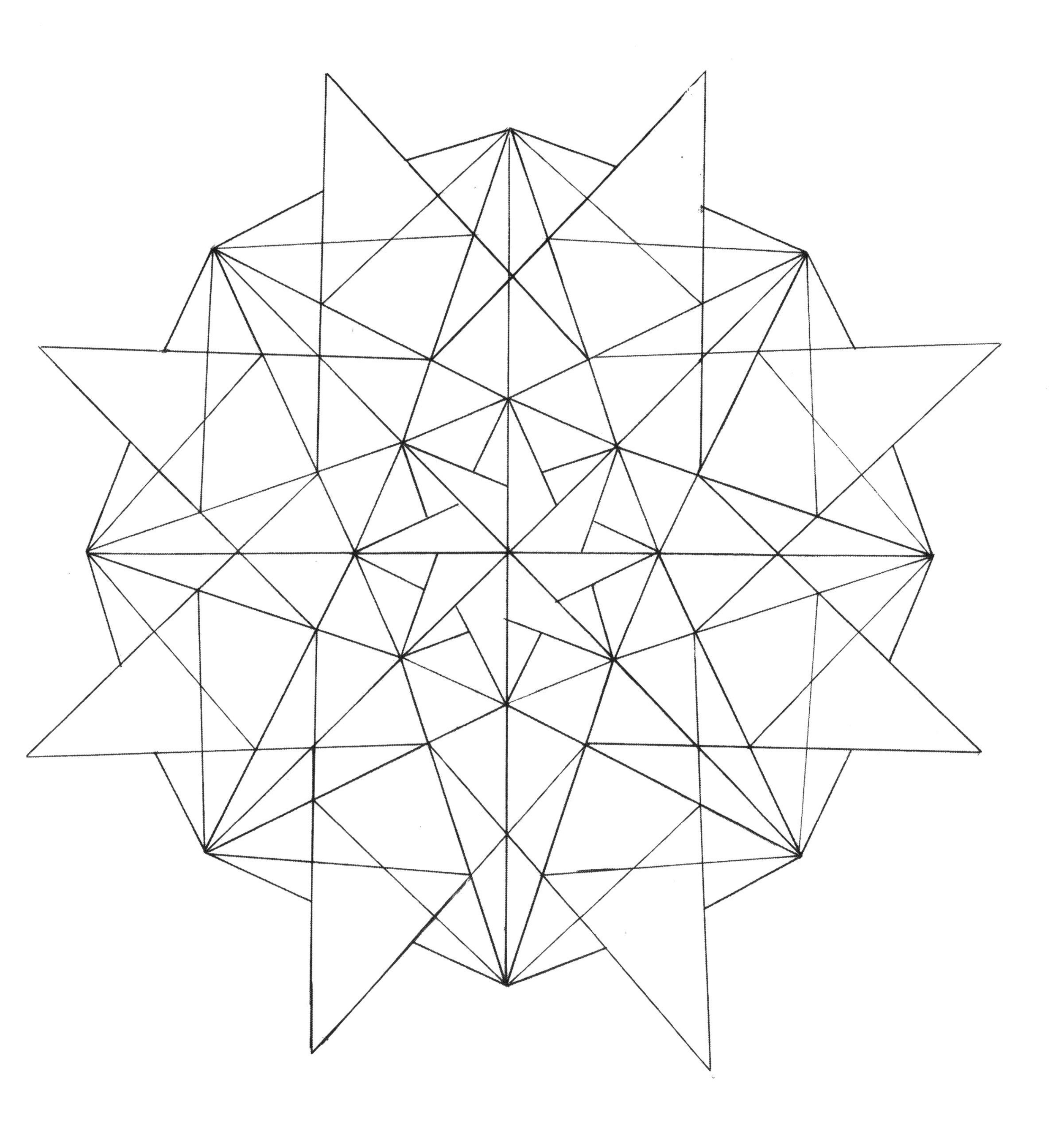

#4, Rahu

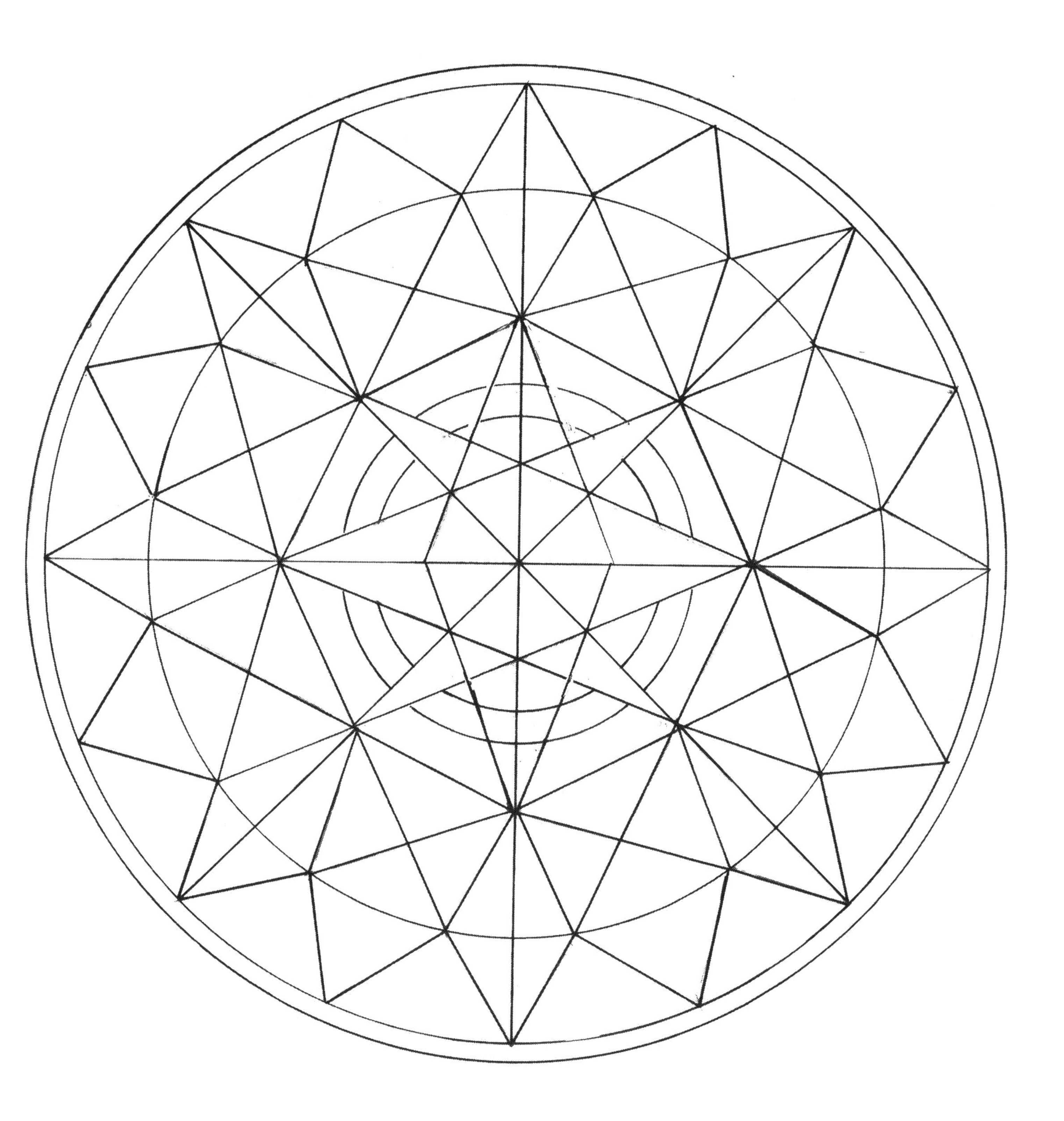

#5, Mercury

#6, Venus

#7, Ketu

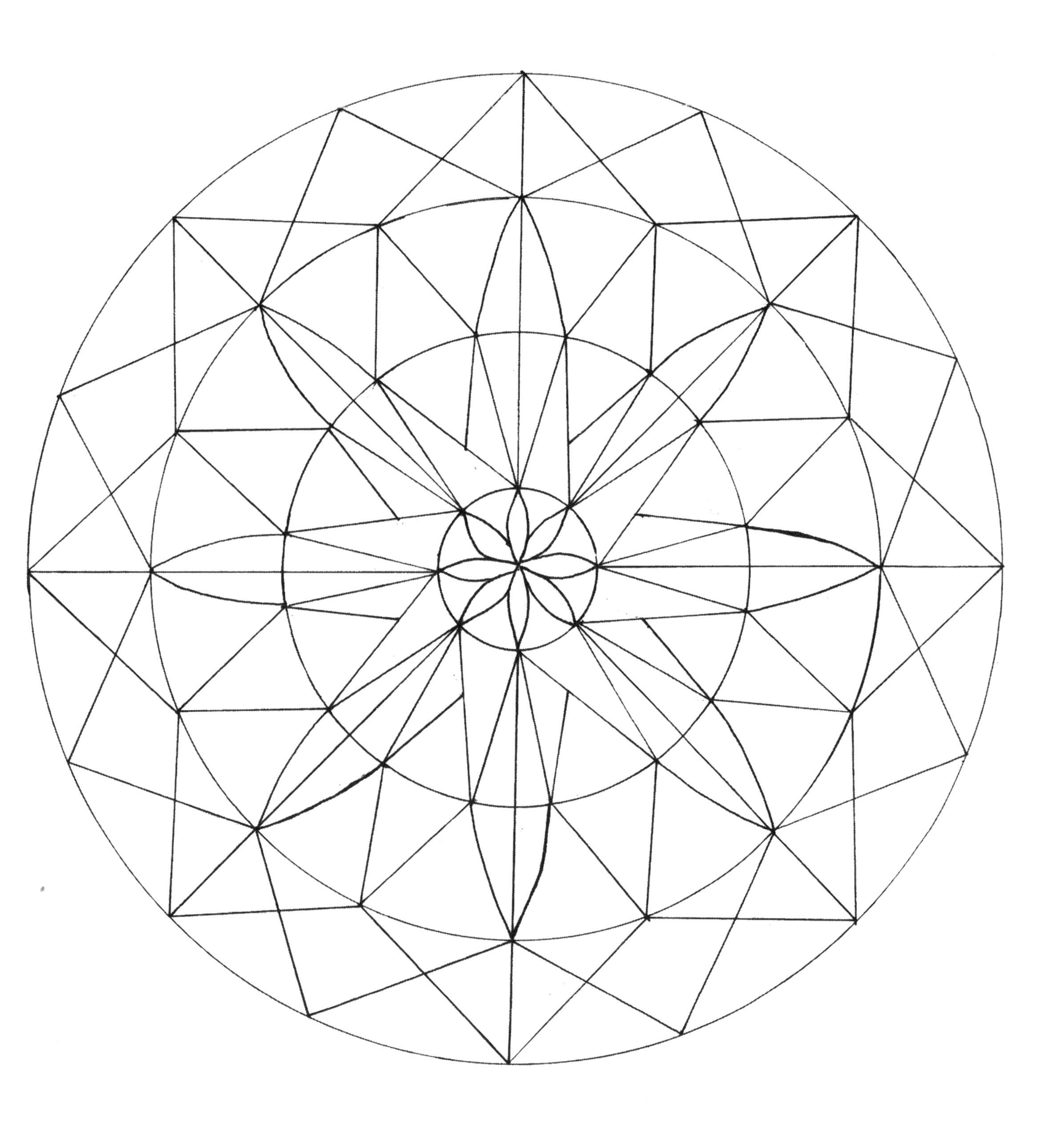

#8, Saturn

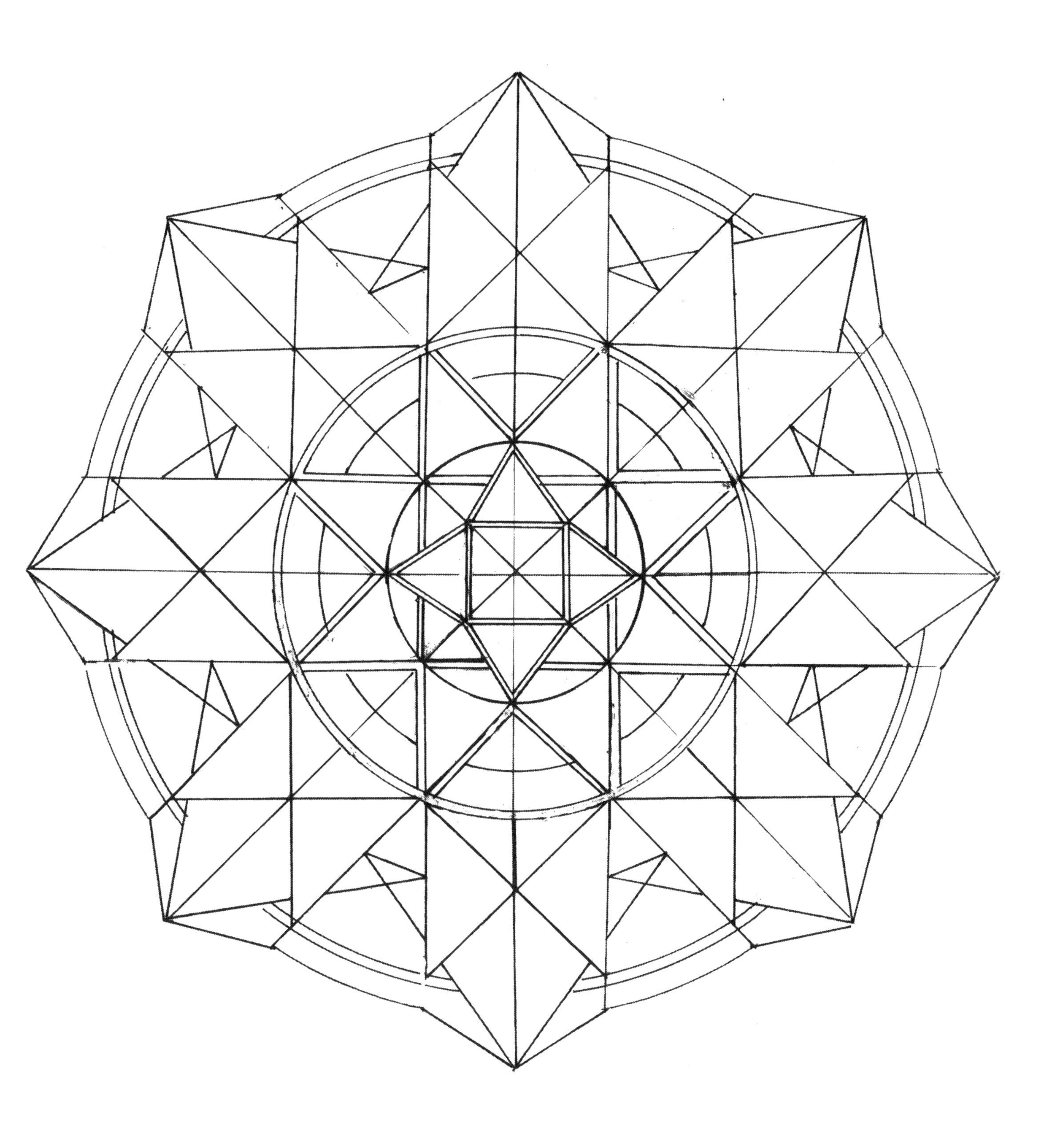

#9, Mars

Made in United States
Orlando, FL
27 January 2024